Toys for Roy

By Cameron Macintosh

"Here, Roy!" said Jim.
"Let's play with your toy."

Jim threw a toy, but Roy did not leap at it.

Now the owl has a safe house!

CHECKING FOR MEANING

1. Who was going to help make a new tower? *(Literal)*

2. What did the owl catch when it went hunting? *(Literal)*

3. Why do you think the owl did not go in the new house at first? *(Inferential)*

EXTENDING VOCABULARY

tower	How would you describe the *tower* in the book? What other words could you use to describe a tower?
frown	What is the meaning of the word *frown*? What is the opposite of *frown*?
mouse	What is a *mouse*? Where do mice usually live? What other word in the book rhymes with *mouse*?

MOVING BEYOND THE TEXT

1. Why do you think the owl chose to nest in the tower?

2. Where else do birds build nests?

3. What do birds make nests out of?

4. What might the new tower that Dad helped build have looked like?

DIPHTHONGS

PRACTICE WORDS

tower

town

owl

down

house

frown

out

mouse

mouth

How

Now

Wow

Jim got Roy's fish toy.

It flopped across the deck,
but Roy did not jump at it.

"Come on, boy!" said Jim.

He pointed at the toy.

But Roy did not get up.

"Mum," said Jim.

"Roy gets no joy from his toys!"

"Roy can not see his toys well," said Mum.

"Can we get a toy that Roy can play with?" said Jim.

Mum and Jim went to
the pet shop.

"We need a toy for a dog
who can not see well," said Jim.

The lady pointed up.

"I have two toys your dog
will enjoy!" she said.

At home, Jim ran to see Roy.

"Come and join us, Roy!"
he yelled.
"We have two great toys for you!"

Jim squeezed the first toy.

Oink! Oink!

Roy ran to get the pig.

"He can track the *oink*!" said Jim.

Oink!

Jim put some treats
in the next toy.

He rolled it across the room.

Sniff! Sniff!

"Roy can track the smell!" said Jim.

Roy tapped the toy, and a treat fell out!

He tapped at the toy again and again.

Roy played with both toys all day long.

"Roy enjoys his toys!" said Jim.

"We spoil him!" said Mum.

CHECKING FOR MEANING

1. Where do Jim and Mum go to look for toys for Roy? *(Literal)*

2. What toys do they buy for Roy? *(Literal)*

3. Why did Roy enjoy his new toys? *(Inferential)*

EXTENDING VOCABULARY

pointed	What did Jim do when he *pointed* at the toy? What other meaning can the word *pointed* have? E.g. a pointed hat.
to, two	The words *to* and *two* sound the same. What does *two* mean? How is it different from *to*? What might help you remember the difference between the words?
enjoys	What is the base of *enjoys*? How does adding an s change the meaning of the base? What other words or phrases have a similar meaning to *enjoy*? E.g. like, have fun.

MOVING BEYOND THE TEXT

1. What toys do you like playing with? Why?

2. Are your toys suitable for pets to play with?

3. What else might you have to think about if you had a pet that couldn't see well?

4. What do we do to look after people who can't see well?

DIPHTHONGS

| oy | ow | oo | aw |

PRACTICE WORDS

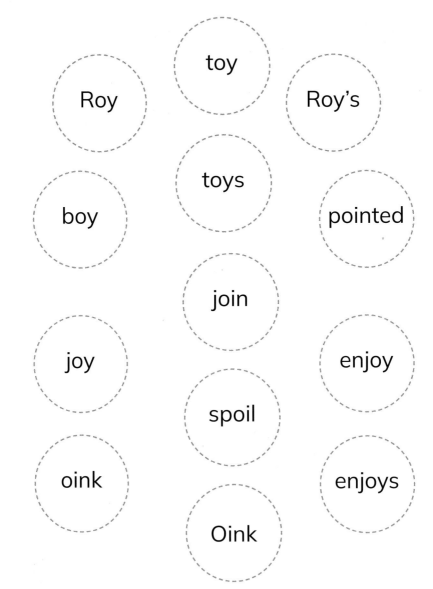

Roy

toy

Roy's

boy

toys

pointed

join

joy

enjoy

spoil

oink

enjoys

Oink